APPLYING REVERSE PSYCHOLOGY

Enhance Your Sex Appeal and Social Standing

By

Stefan Cain

Contents

About the Author 6

Welcome to Reverse Psychology...7

Understanding the Basics of Reverse Psychology....................9

    Free Choice and Free Will...9

    Reactance 11

Reverse Psychology as an Interpersonal Influence Technique....14

    Who Uses Reverse Psychology?..14

    Reverse Psychology as Strategic Self-Anticonformity 16

    Reverse Psychology in Everyday Life..19

        Study One...20

        Study Two 22

Reverse Psychology and the Uncertainty Principle.................26

    The Uncertainty Principle...26

    He Loves Me, He Loves Me Not..27

    Why Is Uncertainty Attractive?...29

The Science of Playing (Moderately) Hard to Get...................31

    Emotional Intensity and Motivation..31

    Emotional Intensity and Romantic Attraction................................32

    Can Playing Hard to Get Make You More Attractive? 34

        Study One...36

        Study Two 38

When to Play (Moderately) Hard to Get..................................42

When Does Playing Hard to Get Increase Romantic Attraction? 42
    Study One..45
    Study Two 47
Using Reverse Psychology to Attract a New Romantic Partner...52
    Step 1: Establishing Commitment..52
        Assess the Situation..53
        Make an Impression..54
        The Art of Conversation 57
        Make Yourself Memorable 59
        Sealing the Deal 62
    Step 2: Playing Hard to Get 63
        The Waiting Game..64
        Avoiding the Friend Zone 64
        Sending Mixed Signals..66
        Maintaining Uncertainty 68
        Make Yourself Scarce 69
        Make Them Chase You...70
        Take Things Slow 72
    One Night Stands..73
Using Reverse Psychology to Re-Attract Your Ex....................77
A Final Word..…..............80

This page intentionally left blank

All rights reserved. No part of this publication may be reproduced, distributed, or transmitted in any form or by any means, including photocopying, recording, or other electronic or mechanical methods, without the prior written permission of the publisher, except in the case of brief quotations embodied in critical reviews and certain other noncommercial uses permitted by copyright law.

Copyright © 2015 by Stefan Cain

Although the author and publisher have made every effort to ensure that the information in this book was correct at press time, the author and publisher do not assume and hereby disclaim any liability to any party for any loss, damage, or disruption caused by errors or omissions, whether such errors or omissions result from negligence, accident, or any other cause.

About the Author

Stefan Cain has spent the majority of his working career in numerous academic research positions, working on a wealth of psychological, societal and cultural topics. His research work and adept studies have been used to form the backbone of many popular titles available today, providing him with the experience and hunger to delve deeper into some avenues of thought.

Alongside his serious academic work, Stefan has been published in a number of prominent publications; filing news reports, features and insightful opinion pieces on myriad topics throughout his career. It was here, in this capacity as a journalist, that he first began to take conscious note of human behaviors and the science behind it.

With his background in psychological studies, Stefan delves right into a popular, yet underestimated social phenomenon known as reverse psychology. In this book, he presents to you the science behind it, as well as practical ways to use it to your advantage in everyday life.

Welcome to Reverse Psychology

Remember when that one boy or girl who wouldn't stop teasing you in grade school? Inevitably, some adult must have laughed and told you that they were only teasing you because they liked you. You were probably more than a little confused. Why would someone tease you if they actually liked you?

Looking back, it still probably seems counter-intuitive and maybe even a little mysterious. People appreciate honesty, so if someone likes you it makes sense that they would just tell you. And if you like them, the best way to win their attraction is to be honest about your feelings for them, right?

Wrong. As you probably know all too well, human psychology—the psychology of dating and attraction in particular—is inexplicably complicated. Inherent, often subconscious, drives and desires influence our actions in such a way that we tend to act in ways that can seem less than rational.

This book attempts to help you understand the way in which these subconscious drives have shaped certain aspects of the human mind. Specifically, it seeks to help you understand the psychological nuance of the interpersonal influence known as reverse psychology, as well as how you can use reverse psychology to influence members of the opposite sex to be attracted to you.

The first chapter offers a basic overview of reverse psychology—what it is, and why, on a psychological level, it works. The second chapter explores the way in which reverse psychology functions as an effective interpersonal influence technique. The third chapter seeks to link reverse psychology to something called the uncertainty principle. Social psychologists have determined that it is actually more attractive to display a *lack* of interest in a person than it is to demonstrate that you are attracted to them.

From here, the book proceeds into a discussion of the dating technique known as playing hard to get. This strategy is inextricably linked to reverse psychology—specifically the uncertainty principle. The fourth chapter seeks to explain, on a psychological level, why playing hard to get is so often an effective dating strategy, while the fifth chapter clarifies the psychological conditions that are necessary in order to succeed at playing hard to get.

The sixth and seventh chapters are oriented towards application. In the sixth chapter, you will learn everything you need to know about how to attract a new romantic partner by playing hard to get. The seventh chapter offers information about how you can use a modification of the same strategy in order to win back a previous romantic partner.

By the time you finish this book, you will know how reverse psychology works, how it applies to the context of attraction, and, most importantly, how you can effectively use it to win the attraction of a member of the opposite sex.

Understanding the Basics of Reverse Psychology

If you're reading this book, you want to know how to attract someone by using reverse psychology. Out of all the potential romantic partners they could possibly choose, you wish to learn about a technique you can use to make sure that your desired partner chooses *you*.

Free Choice and Free Will

Before you can truly understand how you can make someone attracted to you by using reverse psychology, you will need to understand what reverse psychology is, and in order for you to fully understand what reverse psychology is, you will first need to understand a few basics about the mechanism of choice.

Social psychologists have found that there are several key features that factor into the process of choice. The first step towards making any decision is to narrow down a vast range of choices to a select few. This step tends to happen rather quickly—out of the billions of potential romantic partners a man or woman may select, they will inevitably discard the majority and hone in on a just a few select options.

There is some inherent risk in discarding so many potential options so quickly—it is, unfortunately, possible for someone who would have actually been quite attractive to be rejected solely because the person doing the choosing did not consider them carefully enough. Still, the human mind can only deal with a large set of possible choices by quickly eliminating all but a few of them.

The second step in the mechanism of choice involves a more careful consideration of the limited choices that remain. It is often the prevailing assumption that most people look at each potential romantic partner and perform some kind of rational cost-benefit analysis—that is, they look at both the potential good and bad aspects of each potential partner, adding up these positives and negatives, and choose the person with the greatest net sum.

Most people, however, are not entirely rational. Their decisions are subject to errors, biases, and a number of other influencing factors. Reverse psychology, as you will soon learn, is a form of social influence that you can use in order to persuade them to choose you over any other romantic partners they may have been considering.

Though everyone has to make all kinds of choices, they tend to postpone choices having to do with important decisions—such as choosing a potential romantic partner. This deferral of choice is called decision avoidance. Often, people defer a choice because they fear that they will experience some kind of regret. It is, in other words, natural to avoid making a choice that could lead to taking any action that could later come to seem regrettable.

In fact, most people are so afraid of choosing an option they may later regret, that they tend to anticipate feeling more regret by choosing to do something than they fear the amount of regret they will experience by choosing to do nothing at all, even though choosing to do nothing is a choice in its own right. People therefore tend to be overwhelmed by the prospect of decision making—they simply find it too difficult.

The more options there are to choose from, the more frightened people tend to be of actually making a choice. As more and more options become available, it becomes more and more difficult to recognize which one is the best choice—so much so that the fear of potential regret often intensifies dramatically given an increase in the number of available options.

Interestingly, however, eliminating most of the options will not eliminate the fear of potential regret. When offered too few options, people instead begin to fear that none of the available choices will be good enough. Thus people, then, have an interest in preserving their options.

Reactance

The idea that people are inherently committed to preserving their options is the central point in an important and well-esteemed psychological theory known formally as reactance theory. Reactance theory refers to a theory known to most as reverse psychology.

Reactance theory or reverse psychology is rooted in the notion that people strongly desire to have freedom of choice. Accordingly, people will experience a negative reaction—called reactance—when they feel as though something or someone outside of themselves is limiting their options.

Reactance—the negative emotion people feel when they believe that their freedom has been reduced—typically catalyzes a specific two-tiered response.

First, the person experiencing reactance will find the forbidden option more attractive. They will desire it more than they would if it weren't off limits to them. If someone who was considering you as a potential romantic partner were to believe that you were, for some reason, unobtainable to them as a romantic partner, they will suddenly find themselves thinking that you are more attractive than any romantic partner that is still available to them.

Second, the person experiencing reactance will take steps to reassert their freedom by attempting to reclaim the option they believe has been lost to them. Someone who believes that you are unavailable to them as a romantic partner would thus actively begin trying to win your attraction.

Reverse psychology has been studied in a number of different contexts and proven to work well in them all.

In one study, two-year-olds who were instructed not to play with a certain toy suddenly found that the forbidden toy was much more appealing and were markedly more likely to sneak over and play with it when they felt like no one was watching.

In another study, students were told that they could have their choice between five posters, but after they had chosen, they were told that one of the posters was no longer available. Even if the unavailable poster had originally been their third choice, many students suddenly decided that they posted they couldn't have was the poster they liked most and expressed regret that they could not have it.

Those labels that warn you, the potential consumer, about potentially objectionable material in TV programs, films, video games, comics, and music have been proven to have an effect opposite to that which was intended—the more "forbidden" the media in question appears, the more it will likely tend interest you.

Finally, those who had considered having sex with a particular person have been proven to grow far more coercive after that person has rejected their advances.

Reverse psychology is inextricably linked to broader issues of free will and freedom of action. People are inherently sensitive to how much freedom of choice they have and they are—often subconsciously—driven by an innate desire to gain and preserve their options.

When you make it seem as though a person's options have been externally limited, you will naturally evoke within them a feeling of reactance. Often, this feeling of reactance will be so strong that it will make a person irresistibly attracted to the person whom they believe is unavailable to them.

In short, the ultimate trick to attracting a romantic partner is to make the person you desire think that they can't have you.

Reverse Psychology as an Interpersonal Influence Technique

Perhaps at this point you're thinking that using reverse psychology to attract someone may seem insincere or even a bit manipulative. This could not be further from the truth. When you employ reverse psychology, you're simply recognizing the fact that people are naturally inclined to want what they can't have.

The truth is that reverse psychology is just one of the many social influence techniques that people use all the time. In fact, you'd be hard-pressed to find someone who hasn't used reverse psychology as a social influence tactic in one context or another.

There's no reason to feel bad about using reverse psychology to influence someone to be attracted to you. Given both the efficacy of reverse psychology and the frequency with which people report to using reverse psychology to influence others, you would be putting yourself at a competitive disadvantage by *not* using reverse psychology to attract a member of the opposite sex!

Who Uses Reverse Psychology?

That many people use reverse psychology and use it effectively is a proven fact. In 2011, three esteemed psychologists conducted a study in which they sought to answer a simple question—do people use reverse psychology? Three renowned psychologists—Geoff MacDonald, Paul Nail, and Jesse Harper—wanted to study what they called the compliance paradigm, which is a term they used to describe what happens when an individual makes a direct request to another individual. MacDonald, Nail, and Harper were especially interested in how the compliance paradigm worked when the individual making the request was of equal or lower status than the person receiving the request.

Macdonald, Nail, and Harper took note of number of influence techniques involving the compliance paradigm which had been shown by previous studies to be quite effective. Among these techniques were the "foot in the door" (FITD) technique, wherein the requester asks for something minor in order to increase compliance with a later, larger request, the "door in the face" (DITF) technique in which the influencer uses a person's noncompliance with an initiatory large request in order to increase his compliance with an immediate, smaller request, and a technique known as "disrupt-then-reframe" (DTR), in which the requester phrases his request in unconventional terms and, when asked to clarify, reframes his request in terms meant to seem advantageous to the source of influence.

MacDonald, Nail, and Harper wanted to know how reverse psychology—a social influence technique that had hitherto been largely neglected in psychological study—compared to these tried-and-true social influence techniques. For the purpose of their research, MacDonald, Nail, and Harper referred to reverse psychology as strategic self-anticonformity (SSA).

Reverse Psychology as Strategic Self-Anticonformity

To engage in strategic self-anticonformity is to strategically anticipate that the person you wish to influence does not like to be told what to do and, accordingly, to attempt to influence them by making a request opposite of what you truly desire. Strategic self-anticonformity is simply another formal name for reverse psychology.

MacDonald, Nail, and Harper hypothesized that reverse psychology would most likely be employed when a source of influence expects negativity, disagreeableness, or contradiction from the target he or she wishes to influence. Given that most people tend to be quite disagreeable when they feel as though they're being told what to do, MacDonald, Nail, and Harper expected to find that people employed reverse psychology with some frequency.

Indeed MacDonald, Nail, and Harper cite reactance theory, stating that an individual who perceives that their options are being externally limited will experience enough discomfort that they will be motivated to re-establish that freedom by refusing to comply with any influence attempts.

Whenever someone seems inclined to respond with reactance, note MacDonald, Nail, and Harper, you should be able to successfully be able to influence that person to do what you desire them to do by misrepresenting your desires. In stating a desire opposite to that of your genuine desire, you make the logical assumption that the person you wish to influence will reject your stated desire and attempt to do the opposite. This,

MacDonald, Nail, and Harper claim, will result in that person acting in accordance with your genuine (but unstated!) desire.

As an example, MacDonald, Nail, and Harper propose a situation in which parents pretend to be displeased with their child's choice of romantic partner in the (secret) hopes that their displayed lack of support will actually support their child's relationship.

Given the hypothesized effectiveness of reverse psychology in many real world contexts, MacDonald, Nail, and Harper conducted a scientific study in order to see whether reverse psychology was, in fact, a genuine, real world influence technique. If it was, they also wished to compare the frequency people reportedly used reverse psychology with the frequency with which people reported using the previously established influence techniques—specifically, the techniques known as "foot in the door" (FITD), "door in the face" (DITF), and "define then reframe" (DTR).

According to Macdonald, Nail, and Harper, reverse psychology is different from these other social influence techniques because it is a relatively indirect form of influence. Given someone who is known to be generally agreeable, direct influence strategies—a suggestion accompanied by strong supporting arguments—should be enough to get them to comply with you.

As long as the people you wish to influence are agreeable, they will likely agree with your suggestion unless they genuinely have another option they would prefer to pursue and can offer superior arguments that are able to counter your arguments. The strategy of genuinely stating your desires is referred to as "self-conformity," because you are anticipating that the influence target will be agreeable and cooperative, which makes it possible for you to present a suggestion that is in self-conformity to (i.e. consistent with) your true desires.

Whenever the influence target expresses a clear desire for dominance and control over his or her options—as most people are naturally inclined to do—a self-conformity influence strategy is liable to fail. It is at this point that it becomes advantageous for you to employ strategic self-anticonformity, i.e. reverse psychology.

If you were to disclose his or her true preferences as to what you would like the person you desire to do, it is highly likely that the person you wish to attract would state an opposing desire. Stubbornly, they will refuse to comply with your own desire because they feel as though to do so would be to limit their freedom of choice.

It makes sense, therefore, for you to propose a suggestion that is the opposite of what you actually want someone to do. Then, when the influence target expresses his desire to do the opposite, you can simply give a spirited but entirely facetious defense against your original suggestion.

Eventually, you will "concede" to the self-stated desires of the person you're seeking to influence, as what they desire will now be in accordance with whatever you *genuinely* desire. The person you're trying to influence will never know that they are actually doing what you wanted them to do in the first place; instead, they will believe that they are re-establishing their own free will. Both parties will come away feeling good about the outcome of the situation.

Reverse Psychology in Everyday Life

Macdonald, Nail, and Harper had noticed that reverse psychology was familiar within the realm of pop culture, but absent in scientific literature. No one had researched its pervasiveness or its effectiveness in everyday life.

Still, they were able to compile a wealth of anecdotal evidence about the pervasiveness of reverse psychology as a social influence technique. For example, the researchers cite the autobiography of country music singer/songwriter Mel Tillis, who writes that his father had a tendency to be "endlessly contrary" towards his mother.

Tillis' father would always disagree with what Tillis' mother wanted, even if he had no apparent reason to. If Tillis' mother wanted to go out for barbecue, for example, his father would insist upon taking her to a Mexican restaurant (and vice versa). Tills recalls the way in which his mother eventually learned how to say the opposite of her true choice so that his father would characteristically disagree (anticonform), thereby allowing his mother to eat where she had initially desired.

Given the limited and unscientific nature of anecdotal evidence, Macdonald, Nail, and Harper set out to gather scientific evidence that would allow them to determine the way in which average people used reverse psychology as an influence technique.

Study One

In their first study, Macdonald, Nail, and Harper invited 159 university students from the University of Queensland to participate in a study about their interactions with others. They gave a few examples of times in which people may say the opposite of what they believe in an attempt to get other people to agree with them—a mother who expressed her distaste for her daughter's new boyfriend in an attempt to increase her daughter's attraction to him and a person who says they look unattractive in the hopes of getting others to disagree and praise their appearance—and then asked the study's participants to write about a description of a time they tried to get someone to agree with them or do something they wanted to do by advocating the opposite.

The participants were asked not to limit themselves to situations that were just like the examples given. In fact, they were encouraged to come up with a situation that was markedly different from the given examples. Those who could not come up with an example were asked to leave the section blank. After giving their own examples, participants were asked to asked to rate (using a scale of 1-9) how difficult it was for them to come up with an example, how successful they were in getting the person they mentioned to agree with them, and how frequently they would use the tactic of saying the opposite of what they wanted in order to get others to agree or comply with them (in this case, 1 = never, 5 = once every two months, 9 = once per day).

The results of MacDonald, Nail, and Harper's first study were staggering. Of the 159 people who participated, over 91%

were able to offer an example of how they used reverse psychology to get others to comply with them. These examples were then evaluated by two independent raters in order to determine whether the 137 examples given were valid instances of SSA; in 105 cases, both raters concluded that the examples were valid. In 17 cases, the raters could not agree on the validity of the example.

Among the unanimously valid responses, one respondent said that when "there is a choice between doing two things with a friend, I have told the other person to make the choice, hoping / knowing that they'd disagree and tell me I could choose (so I'd get my choice without looking too controlling)." Another admitted to telling his ex-girlfriend that he didn't need her anymore in order to get her to disagree and say that she did.

Of those participants who were judged by both raters to have offered a valid response, the average reported difficulty of employing reverse psychology was 4.42 (with 9.0 representing no difficulty whatsoever). The average success rate of the task was reported to be 6.60 (with 9.0 representing complete success). Finally, the average frequency with which participants reported that the used the SSA tactic was 5.41—approximately once every month and a half.

The results of this study prove that people in the real world most definitely do use reverse psychology as a social influence tactic and that they are willing to do so quite frequently.

Though MacDonald, Nail, and Harper confirmed that the use of reverse psychology was fairly prevalent, the researchers felt that their confidence in preliminary conclusion was limited due to the lack of a standard of comparison. For this reason, they conducted a second study in which they attempted to contextualize the prevalence of reverse psychology by comparing the use of reverse psychology as an influence strategy to the use of other, already well-researched strategies.

Study Two

Thus in their second study, they asked 69 participants to provide an example of the two forms of reverse psychology which had been identified in their first study, as well as examples of the other social influence tactics FITD, DITF, and DTR.

Participants were given a description of each tactic, with each description followed by a brief example. Then, participants were asked to provide an example of a time when they themselves had employed the same influence tactic. Once again, participants were asked to rate how difficult it was to come up with an example, how successful they were in influencing their influence target, and how frequently they employed that tactic in their everyday life. The participants examples of persuasive strategic self-anticonformity (PSSA) were unanimously declared to be valid in 26 cases (7 cases were contested); for reassurance strategic anticonformity (RSSA), 50 cases were unanimously deemed valid (8 cases were contested).

The results of the second study appeared to confirm the real-world relevance of reverse psychology that was implied by the first study. 72% of the participants in the study were able to provide valid examples of RSSA, while 38% were able to provide valid examples of PSSA. However, the percentage of participants who were able to provide PSSA was approximately the same as the percentage of participants who were able to provide valid examples of previously-established influence tactics—this suggests that PSSA does occur with some regularity in real world influence scenarios.

According to MacDonald, Neil, and Harper, the combined results of both studies suggest that reverse psychology is an exceedingly valid influence tactic that is very much deserving of closer studies by social influence researchers.

The vast majority of those who participated in the study were able to provide an example of a time when they used reverse psychology in their own lives; moreover, they were able to do so at a rate comparable to the rate at which they utilized other influence tactics that have already been established in psychological literature.

Given the nature of participants' responses, MacDonald, Neil, and Harper also found that reverse psychology is particularly useful when it comes to gaining reassurance and affirmation from others, as the inherently indirect nature of reverse psychology makes it particularly useful for sensitive interpersonal contexts.

MacDonald, Neil, and Harper warn, however, that while reverse psychology seems be relatively successful as an influence technique, it carries inherent risks. The form of reverse psychology they call RSSA is especially liable to backfire, as it is quite possible that the person you wish to influence could agree with you when you present a negative self-view that you had hoped they would refute.

Of course, PSSA also has the potential to backfire on the influence source if the influence target agrees with the influence source's original, disingenuous request; however, people have been known to be quite good at tacit coordination—they can anticipate the behavior of others and adjust their own actions accordingly. Therefore, the rate at which PSSA backfires may actually be quite low.

Still, even successful PSSA can have some unpleasant consequences. The most obvious of these are the imposition of unequal power dynamics (through the intentional withholding of information) and lingering feelings of inauthenticity. Thus, while PSSA is indeed a reliable way to gain influence over a target who would likely otherwise offer resistance, that success requires willfully misdirecting the influence target—this may ultimately cause the influence target to experience feelings of dissatisfaction and perhaps even guilt.

At the end of their study, MacDonald, Neil, and Harper conclude that reverse psychology seems to be a relevant, real world influence tactic; however, they do note that further research is needed to expand upon the dynamics of reverse psychology as a form of influence. As they conducted a study that gathered information via self-report, MacDonald, Neil, and Harper note that there would be value in conducting a study of reverse psychology that used either observational or experimental methods.

They propose one such potential study in which participants would be asked to influence a research confederate who is consistently either agreeable or disagreeable. In such a study, MacDonald, Neil, and Harper hypothesize that—based on the results of their own studies of reverse psychology—given multiple attempts to influence the target, participants would eventually begin employing reverse psychology in order to succeed in influencing their disagreeable target. If they did, MacDonald, Neil, and Harper believe that this study would confirm that anticonformity naturally promotes a response of self-anticonformity—i.e. that we naturally use reverse psychology on those who we expect will be disagreeable.

Based on this research, people in the real world really do use reverse psychology—and it tends to work quite well! As MacDonald, Neil, and Harper's study confirms, it's not at all unusual for people in real-world social influence situations—especially those of an intrapersonal nature—to use reverse psychology as a form of influence.

Every day, there are plenty of people in the real world who readily choose to employ reverse psychology as an influence strategy because they know that it is a powerful influence tactic that they can use to sway even—especially—those who would be most disagreeable.

Reverse Psychology and the Uncertainty Principle

In his esteemed manual *The Art of Seduction*, Robert Green writes that whenever you give off an "elusive, enigmatic aura," you make people want to know more and draw them into your circle. Green warns that the moment people feel like they know what to expect from you, "your spell on them is broken." In practice, is that while people will like you if you like them, they will find people you more attractive when they don't know whether you like them or not.

The Uncertainty Principle

Whenever someone receives clear signals of interest from you, they will be momentarily pleased. Soon, however, they will internalize and adapt to the knowledge that you like them. Soon, they'll begin to lose interest in you.

But when someone is uncertain whether you're interested in them or not, they won't be able to stop thinking about you. People tend to be insecure when it comes to what others think of them, so when someone doesn't know what you think of them, they will tend to fear that you uninterested—and therefore unavailable.

Your imagined unavailability will therefore trigger a reactance response. The person who thinks that you may be uninterested in them will be so preoccupied with your perceived lack of interest that they will scarcely be able to think of anyone else, let alone anyone who has expressed an obvious interest in them.

Eventually, it's natural for them to begin to interpret their constant thoughts about you as a sign of attraction—after all, if they can't stop thinking about you, they must really like you! Every time they finds themselves fearing that you loves them not, they are that much closer to realizing their attraction to you!

He Loves Me, He Loves Me Not...

The allure of uncertainty has been affirmed in a study conducted by Erin Whitchurch. Whitchurch sought to discover which was a more potent recipe for seduction—the reciprocity principle (the principle that people like those who like them) or the uncertainty principle (people like those who *might* like them).

In her study of 47 female undergraduates, Whitchurch and her colleagues told each woman that a number of male students had viewed her Facebook page and rated how much he'd like to get to know her. One group of these women was informed that they would be meeting the four men who had given them the highest ratings; another, the four men who had given them an average rating. But the final group of women were told that that the extent to which each of the four men liked her was unknown.

After briefing the participants about how much the men were interest in them, Whitchurch showed all of the women four fake profiles of attractive male college students. Once the women had viewed these profiles, Whitchurch asked them to report their mood and several aspects of their attraction to the fictional male college students. Fifteen minutes later, Whitchurch asked the students to report their mood again, as well as the extent to which thoughts about the men in question had popped into their head during the prior fifteen minutes.

The results were undeniable—uncertainty and unavailability are incredibly attractive. Whitchurch did find some evidence of the reciprocity principle. The women studied reported that they liked the men whom they were led to believe really liked them more than they liked the men who they believed only liked them an average amount.

Most attractive to the women, however, were the men who were believed to be uncertain in regards to their feelings about the women. Indeed, it was the men of uncertain opinion whom the women reported thinking about most frequently.

Furthermore, there was some evidence to suggest that this high level of attraction was indeed caused by the frequency of these thoughts; thus, it was the uncertainty itself that the women found attractive, but the frequency of the thoughts that this uncertainty induced.

Of course, women in the liked-best category reported that they experienced a more positive mood than the women in the liked-average category; however, there was no statistically significant difference between the moods of the women who were liked the most and the moods of the women who were in the unknown category. Women felt just as positive when they had no idea how much the men liked them as they did when they knew for sure that the men liked them.

Whitchurch's study was groundbreaking, as it was the first study to manipulate different degrees of certainty in order to observe the effects of certainty on attraction. In that sense, her study sheds new light on the seduction tactic known as playing hard to get. Making yourself seem as though you are unavailable may in fact make you seem more attractive.

As Whitchurch conclusively declares at the end of her study, "People who create uncertainty about how much they like someone can increase that person's interest in them." As far as initial attraction is concerned, the allure of the unknown is a potent force."

Why Is Uncertainty Attractive?

Reviewing Whitchurch's study, Anthony Servadio proposes that our tendency to be attracted to uncertainty is Freudian in nature. Freud theorized that deep within everyone's subconscious resides their inner child and that this inner child can have a powerful influence on the way in which a person behaves.

Low self-esteem typically develops at some point between the time a child turns six to the time he or she turns fourteen—a period known as middle childhood. Any child who does not master social competency during this period will likely struggle with lifelong feelings of inferiority and low self-esteem. Any insecurities that develop during this period come to be buried deeply within a person's subconscious, and they can often come to be powerful motivating factors when it comes to a person's behavior.

Women especially are vulnerable to insecurities about their attractiveness—one study conducted by Dove found that only 4% of women considered themselves to be beautiful. According to Servadio, it is these deep-rooted insecurities that may be the key to understanding why it is better for you to remain ambiguous about your attraction to a potential new partner.

Given the insecurities that riddle 96% of women—and doubtless a large percentage of men, it is likely that someone will respond to your immediate, obvious, enthusiastic attraction by feeling as though there is something "wrong" with that person for being attracted to them. This response coupled with the reactance you will instill by being obvious in your pursuit means that a potential romantic partner is far more likely to be turned off by your obvious attraction.

It is therefore strategically advantageous to employ reverse psychology and make it seem as though you are potentially unavailable—a strategy more popularly known as "playing hard to get."

The Science of Playing (Moderately) Hard to Get

In 1999, social psychologist Jack Brehm proposed that a person's emotions, affect, and mood were motivational states that urged on their behavior towards a given goal. Brehm found that the perceived difficulty of achieving that goal affected the degree of a person's emotional intensity. Whenever someone's goals are inhibited, their degree of emotional intensity (and motivation) will interact with the magnitude of the obstacle to the goal.

Emotional Intensity and Motivation

When there are no obstacles to goal achievement at all, the intensity of a person's experienced emotions will match the potential intensity of emotion and this will represent the importance of achieving the goal in question. The idea sounds more complicated than it actually is. What Brehm was essentially proposing was that people's motivation to achieve a goal will match the anticipated difficulty of that goal. When something is easy, motivation will be low. Increase the difficulty and motivation will increase—to a point. If a goal seems outright impossible, Brehm found that people would become unmotivated once again.

As Brehm puts it, whenever there is a low amount of deterrence, someone is will experience a low level of emotional intensity, as obtaining their goal will only require a small amount of effort. Whenever there is a moderate level of deterrence, the intensity of a person's emotions will rise to the point where the effort needed to obtain the goal matches the degree of importance of that goal. This same principle of emotional intensity and motivation has been seen to apply to feelings of romantic attraction.

Emotional Intensity and Romantic Attraction

Brehm's theory of emotional intensity has been applied to feelings of romantic attraction in a number of psychological studies. In 1984, Wright, Toi, and Breim had male participants rate the attractiveness of potential lab partners after informing them that in order to work with the woman in question, they would have to pass a memory test. These memory tests varied in difficult—easy, medium, and hard—and found that men found the women most attractive when the test was of medium difficulty.

In 1986, Wright and Contrada varied the selectiveness of a potential partner (non-selective, somewhat selective, and extremely selective). Participants in this study found that they were most attracted to the potential partners who were said to be somewhat selective in choosing a romantic partner; potential partners who were not selective and very selective were considered to be far less attractive.

In 1994, Roberson and Wright manipulated men's perception of how difficult (unspecified, easy, somewhat, and impossible) it would be to persuade a woman to be his coworker and concluded that the men had the highest levels of interpersonal attraction to the women who would be somewhat difficult to persuade.

In 2009, Miron, Knepfel, and Parkinson manipulated the importance of a romantic partner's flaws—when the participants in this study were presented with these potential romantic partners, they reported to feel the strongest levels of romantic attraction to the potential partners who had some flaws. Though all of these studies employed a different factor that might have deterred participants from feeling positively towards a potential partner, they all concluded that attraction was at its highest when these flaws posed a moderate deterrent to the goal of forming a partnership.

Given the results of the aforementioned studies, numerous researchers have begun to explore exactly why it is that playing "hard to get" is such an effective dating strategy; however, there have been few studies that have directly tested whether the reciprocity principle has any influence when it comes to functioning as a deterrent and therefore an intensifier of romantic attraction.

Researchers have found that there are different types of attraction and different dimensions to attraction, but regardless of whether attraction is an emotional state or an affective attitudinal component, Brehm hypothesized that someone will be more attracted to a you as a potential romantic partner when they perceive that they will face a moderate degree of resistance in trying to obtain you as their partner.

Thus, reciprocity of attraction may serve as a signal for how difficult it will be to obtain a person as a romantic partner. If this is true, then the partners who seem to be moderately hard to attract will in fact be the most attractive to other individuals, and this may lie at the root of the dating strategy known as playing hard to get.

Can Playing Hard to Get Make You More Attractive?

In light of Whitchurch's study of the uncertainty principle, Stephen Reyson and Iva Miller decided to test whether Brehm's emotional intensity theory could be applied in such a way that the degree to which one reciprocates attraction could be manipulated to serve as a deterrent to romantic attraction. If it could, they believed that this would explain why playing "hard to get" has come to be known as such an effective dating strategy.

Reyson and Miller thus sought to examine the effect of reciprocity of attraction as a deterrent to relationship formation with a potential partner in order to determine whether intentionally withholding the reciprocity of attraction is, in fact, an advantageous dating strategy.

Reyson and Miller hypothesized that a potential partner's degree of reciprocity of attraction could indeed serve as a deterrent to relationship formation and therefore as an intensifier of romantic attraction. They speculated that potential partners who seemed "easy to get" would elicit less attraction than would those who seemed moderately difficult or even hard to get. In other words, they speculated that the relative lack of difficulty of achieving the goal of relationship formation with a potential romantic partner who made him or herself readily available would make that potential romantic partner seem less attractive than someone who did not make themselves so easy to get.

Reyson and Miller conducted two studies in which they asked participants to imagine they were attracted to a coworker who reciprocated their attraction either one (high deterrence), three (moderate deterrence), or five (low deterrence) days per week, or they received no information at all about the coworkers reciprocation of attraction (unspecified deterrence). For the purpose of this study, reciprocity of attraction was defined as the amount as the amount of positive attention the potential partner showed towards the study's participant.

Reyson and Miller believed that, given Brehm's theory of emotional intensity, the potential partner's degree of reciprocity of attraction would influence the participants' intensity of attraction and desire to form a romantic relationship with the potential partner—they hypothesized that participants would be most attracted to the potential partners who displayed a moderate degree of deterrence by showing only a moderate amount of reciprocated attraction.

In other words, Reyson and Miller speculated that participants would be far less attracted to potential partners who showed a high degree of reciprocated attraction than they would be to potential partners who showed only a moderate degree of reciprocated attraction. If a partner barely reciprocated the attraction at all, however, Reyson and Miller hypothesized that the participants would report a low degree of attraction—that is, participants would be just as put off by someone who seemed too hard to get as they would by someone who seemed too easy.

Study One

In the first study, 197 heterosexual students—male and female—were asked to imagine that they were single and attracted to a coworker of the opposite sex, whom they greeted at work every morning. Each participant was given a vignette to read describing the situation they were to imagine: "Every day that you arrive at work, you go straight to the break room for a cup of coffee. An attractive coworker always arrives at the same time and sees you there every morning. Every morning, you try to spark up a conversation with him (her, for male participants)..." Thus, every participant in the study was asked to imagine that he or she was attracted to a coworker to the extent that they felt motivated to converse with them on a daily basis.

After giving this overview of the hypothetical situation, the vignette proceeded in one of four ways. In the control group, no further information was given (i.e. the degree of the coworkers reciprocated attraction was unknown). In the low reciprocity condition, participants were informed that one day each week the coworker to whom they were attracted engaged in great conversation with them, but that (s)he went straight to work on the other four days of the workweek. In the moderate reciprocity condition, participants were informed that their coworker conversed with them three days per week.

In the high reciprocity condition, participants were told that their coworker not only engaged with them in conversation every day of the week, but also hung around their cubicle and often walked the participant to his or her car. After reading one of the four vignettes, participants were asked to complete a twelve item questionnaire in order to measure their attraction to their potential partner. The questions asked how attracted the participant was to their coworker, how pleasant it would be to be with the coworker, how likable they found the coworker, etc.

Contrary to their initial expectations, Reyson and Miller found that the significant effect of manipulation on attraction was marginal. Participants in the unspecified (5.08) and high reciprocity (5.42) conditions indicated near identical levels of attraction to their coworker as a potential romantic partner, whereas those in the moderate reciprocity condition indicated that they were actually slightly less (4.9) attracted to their coworker. As predicted, however, participants in the low reciprocity condition reported that they were very much less attracted (4.03) to their obviously disinterested coworker as a potential romantic partner.

Reyson and Miller were surprised by these results, and concluded that the vignette which depicted the high reciprocity condition did not sufficiently convey the coworker's high degree of reciprocated romantic attraction—that is, he was not portrayed in such a way that he seemed obviously "easy to get." This may have been because his behavior were (mis)interpreted as a cue that he wanted to form a work-related friendship rather than a romantic partnership. In order to test this conclusion, Reyson and Miller designed a second, similar study, in which they increased the displays of the potential partner in the high reciprocity condition. The purpose of this refined second study was to re-examine the effect of varying levels of reciprocated attraction.

Study Two

In this second study, 186 male and female participants followed the same procedure as the participants followed in the first study; however, the vignette shown to those in the high reciprocity condition contained additional displays of obviously romantic attraction on the part of the coworker. In the amended vignette, the coworker was said to join conversations with other coworkers whenever the participant was engaged, involve him or herself in whatever work projects the participant happened to be working on, and call the other participant at home at night just to talk.

These additional displays of attraction were included in the amended vignette in order to more effectively convey the notion that this coworker was inserting him or herself into additional aspects of the participant's life both at work *and* at home. Thus, the vignette about the easy to get coworker was edited so that it more clearly conveyed the extent to which this coworker was interested in forming a romantic relationship with the participant.

After reading the vignettes the participants were once again given twelve questions. These questions asked participants to rate different elements of their degree of attraction to the coworker as a potential romantic partner. These ratings were measured using a scale of one to seven, with one indicating that they were "not at all attracted," and seven indicating that they were "extremely attracted" to the coworker as a potential romantic partner.

The results of this second study were much more in line with the results that Reyson and Miller had originally predicted. Participants in the uncertain condition once again indicated a high degree of attraction (4.86) to the coworker as a potential romantic partner. Participants in the moderate reciprocity condition also found the coworker highly attractive (4.67), as they had in the first study. Those in the low reciprocity condition were again significantly less attracted (3.74) to the coworker as a potential romantic partner.

The most staggering difference between the first and second study, however, was that the participants in the second study in the high reciprocity condition indicated that they found the coworker who was obviously attracted to them to be entirely unattractive (3.34). The coworker who showed a high degree of reciprocated attraction was indeed rated even less attractive than the coworker who hardly reciprocated the participants' attraction at all! Given the amplification of the reciprocated attraction in the high reciprocity condition, the participants indicated that they were much less attracted to the coworker as a potential romantic partner than were the participants in the unspecified and moderate conditions.

Thus, Reyson and Miller concluded that reciprocity of attraction functions effective as a deterrent to romantic attraction in accordance with Brehm's theory of emotional intensity. Though prior studies had supported the idea that attraction towards a potential romantic partner will vary depending on the degree of deterrence to felt attraction, Reyson and Miller's study was the first social influence experiment to test whether the degree of attraction reciprocated could serve as such a detriment to romantic attraction.

Reyson and Miller therefore were able to provide invaluable, compelling evidence that playing somewhat hard to get is a dating technique that can be used to make a person seem more attractive to a potential romantic partner. Participants in Reyson and Miller's study were by far the most attracted to partners who showed a moderate or unknown degree of reciprocated attraction and were significantly less attracted to partners who showed a low degree of reciprocated attraction. They were by far the least attracted, however, to potential partners who demonstrated high degrees of reciprocated attraction.

This may seem counterintuitive—shouldn't we be the most attracted to those who are obviously attracted to us? Not so much, as Reyson and Miller have found. Obvious attraction is, ironically, something that most people tend to find *un*attractive.

In their discussion of the studies' results, Reyson and Miller explore the question of *why* playing (moderately) hard to get makes a person so attractive to potential romantic partners. The answer, they believe, has something to do with the principles of reverse psychology. By establishing an attraction to those potential romantic partners who showed signs of being unattracted to them, participants may have been reacting to the potential loss of freedom to form a relationship with the individuals in both the high and low reciprocity conditions. Their lack of attraction to these potential partners who were obviously trying to form a relationship with them may also be viewed as an expression of reactance.

Thus, even if you do very much desire to form a relationship with someone, it is advantageous to conceal your true intentions and make it seem as though the degree of your attraction to that person is markedly lower than it actually is. By using reverse psychology to make someone believe you are less attracted to them than you actually are, you will, counterintuitively, make yourself attractive to them.

When to Play (Moderately) Hard to Get

At this point you may be feeling a bit skeptical. If all you have to do to attract a member of the opposite sex is appear uninterested in them, wouldn't you always have plenty of men or women falling all over you? And you certainly aren't overwhelmed with attraction for everyone who shows a complete lack of romantic interest in you.

As it turns out, there are certain prerequisite conditions that must be established before you can successfully expect to attract a potential romantic partner with your displayed lack of attraction to them. Thankfully, social psychologists have determined exactly what these prerequisite conditions are and exactly how you can bring them about.

When Does Playing Hard to Get Increase Romantic Attraction?

In 2014, Dai, Dong, and Jia conducted a study called "When Does Playing Hard to Get Increase Romantic Attraction?" In their introduction, Dai, Dong, and Jia note that until recently, prior research on intrapersonal attraction has downplayed the efficacy of the hard-to-get strategy. This is at odds, they claim, with some of the latest research—such as Whitchurch's—which has implied that the hard-to-get strategy does in fact induce greater engagement and motivation to form a relationship with a potential romantic partner.

In their research, Dai, Dong, and Jia attempt to reconcile the reciprocity principle (the idea that we like those who like us) with recent evidence that playing hard to get is a dating strategy proven to be far more effective than being "easy to get" (the idea that we like those who may or may not be attracted to us).

In order to reconcile these seemingly contradictory positions, Dai, Dong, and Jia decompose romantic evaluations into two distinct elements—the element of "liking" and the element of "wanting." Prior to Dai, Dong, and Jia's 2014 research, there had been no studies that empirically explored such a distinction. For their study, Dai, Dong, and Jia thus hypothesized that playing hard to would differentially impact both the element of how much someone "likes" a potential romantic partner and the element of how much someone "wants" a potential romantic partner.

Dai, Dong, and Jia cited recent research in which it has been proven that the brain's reward circuitry governs responses to "liking" something and "wanting" something through separate pathways—for example, the brain can intensely desire any addictive substance without showing any corresponding increase in hedonistic enjoyment. Dai, Dong, and Jia noted that this same phenomenon has been observed with non-addictive rewards: lab rats may be chemically induced to desire glucose, but the strength of their desire does not correlate to the enjoyment they experience upon actually consuming glucose.

Furthermore, Dai, Dong, and Jia cited research which has established that preferences for liking and preferences can not only be separated—they can be driven in altogether opposite directions. In a 2010 study, Litt, Khan, and Shiv found that failure to win a certain prize increased participants' desire for that prize,

43

while simultaneously decreasing the degree to which they liked the prize in subsequent tasks.

A 2011 study conducted by Kim and Labroo confirmed that highlighting incentive value (wanting something) over inherent value (liking something) resulted in the opposite effect on a person's preferred outcome. In other words, it has been established that the more someone wants something, the less they tend to actually like it.

Dai, Dong, and Jia wanted to explore how this distinction between wanting and liking functioned in romantic contexts. They suspected that "hard-to-get" and "easy-to-get" strategies would elicit contrasting motivational and effective responses. Thus, while playing hard to get may be an ineffective way of eliciting a positive effective response (i.e. getting a potential partner to like you), it may nevertheless be a powerful way to elicit a positive motivational response (i.e. getting a potential partner to *want* you).

Dai, Dong, and Jia therefore hypothesized that the motivational benefits of playing hard to get may only apply if there exists some prior psychological commitment—that is, the person you're trying to attract should *like* you at least a little bit before you start playing hard to get in order to get him or her to *want* you.

Dai, Dong, and Jia thus proposed that playing hard to get should work well on a potential partner who is already interested in or committed to the pursuit of future relations, but that it would fail to attract someone who has yet to develop any interest.

A person will be more motivated to achieve the goal of relationship formation, as Reyson and Miller established, when relationship formation is moderately difficult to achieve, but this, of course, can only be true when that person has an active and committed goal in mind—even if only subconsciously.

When a person is not actively committed to a goal, increasing the difficulty of obtaining the goal in question should actually make a person less—rather than more—motivated to achieve it. Moreover, someone is more likely to pursue an endeavor (regardless of difficulty) after they have already invested time and effort into it.

Thus Dai, Dong, and Jia predicted that playing hard to get in romantic attraction would enhance the desire to pursue a potential romantic partner while simultaneously decreasing the likability of that same potential romantic partner; however, they speculated that this asymmetric effect would only occur given the existence of a prior psychological commitment. In the absence of any psychological commitment, playing easy to get would therefore be the superior dating strategy to employ.

Study One

First, Dai, Dong, and Jia tested their hypothesis in a mental simulation. 101 single male college age participants were asked to read a short story in which the participant imagined that he was having lunch with a potential dating partner (whom they refer to as "the player"). Participants received one of two vignettes. In the first, the player was said to be acting relatively responsive (easy to get), whereas in the second, the player was said to be relatively unresponsive (hard to get).

Participants in the hard-to-get condition were informed that the player "responded very passively to the topics [he] initiated, [and] never initiated any topics herself. Additionally, she never smiled at [him] when [they] were sitting together." Conversely, those in the easy-to-get condition were informed that the player responded "very positively to the topics [he] initiated, initiated her own interesting topics from time to time, and kept smiling at [him] throughout the entirety of the lunch." Half of the participants had been asked to imagine their lunch partner was randomly assigned to them; the other half was asked to imagine that their lunch partner was someone on whom they had a crush.

After reading his version of the vignette, each participant was asked to evaluate his lunch partner on both motivational (desirability) and affective (likeability) dimensions. To assess likeability, each participant was asked to report how positive or negative he felt about his lunch partner on a scale of one to nine (1 = very negative, 9 = very positive).

To assess desirability, participants were asked how motivated they were to pursue a romantic relationship with their lunch partner (1 = not at all motivated, 9 = highly motivated). In an attempt to quantify how desirable the participants found their lunch partners, they were also asked how much they would be willing to spend if they were given the opportunity to send her a gift.

As predicted, both those in the no commitment and commitment conditions found the lunch partner in the easy-to-get vignette more likeable (6.32 and 7.72 respectively). In the no-commitment condition, the participant was more inclined to pursue a romantic relationship with the lunch partner who was easy to get; however, in the commitment condition, the partner was more motivated to pursue a relationship with the lunch partner who was playing hard to get.

Thus, despite liking the lunch partner who was playing hard to get less, those who had been previously interested in her showed a much greater desire to form a relationship with her, even in a mere mental simulation of a dating scenario. Dai, Dong, and Jia wanted to confirm the results of their study, so they decided to test them in a real dating context.

<u>Study Two</u>
In their second study, Dai, Dong, and Jai tested the same principles they explored in the first study, only this time they tested them in the context of actual speed dating. Once again, they hypothesized that all participants would find the player who was employing a hard-to-get strategy less likeable than they did the player who was employing the easy-to-get strategy.

Participants who were somehow committed to the player playing hard-to-get, however, would find the player more attractive than they would if she seemed easy to get. Participants who had no commitment to the player, on the other hand, would find the player more attractive if she employed the easy-to-get strategy and less attractive if she employed the hard-to-get strategy.

In order to test this hypothesis, Dai, Dong, and Jai recruited 61 male college students as participants and one female undergraduate student as the confederate for the speed dating. A few days before the speed dating session, the male participants were emailed preparatory information about the study. In this email, participants in the no-commitment condition were given the profile of the dating partner assigned to them (the confederate).

Those in the commitment condition received the same profile, but they also received three bogus profiles and were asked to submit their choice of partner via email. The three fake profiles were designed to be less attractive than the profile of the confederate; thus, each of the participants in the commitment condition chose the confederate as high preferred date.

In order to strengthen the participants' commitment to the confederate, Dai, Dong, and Jai asked them to articulate the reasons the candidate they chose stood out to them—this kind of elaboration has been shown to increase commitment. Next, they instructed those in the commitment condition to send the confederate an email introducing themselves before the speed date. 88% of the participants obliged.

The speed dating study was conducted on a one-to-one basis—in each session, the participant filled out a "pre-date" questionnaire so that the researchers could evaluate his commitment to the dating partner, as well as his expectations of his performance.

After each participant completed this questionnaire, he was escorted to the speed date room. Here, he was permitted to have a five minute conversation with the confederate. The confederate had received clear instructions prior to the dates—she was trained to behave in an obviously responsive or obviously unresponsive manner during her conversation with the male participants.

With those in the easy-to-get condition, the confederate was instructed to try to find a topic of mutual interest, ask the participant some questions in order to show her interest in him, and smile a lot during the five minute conversation. With those in the hard-to-get condition, she was instructed to respond passively to their questions and not ask any questions of her own. She was also told to maintain an unresponsive facial expression and occasionally answer questions with apathetic responses like "I don't care."

After their speed date, participants were ask to fill out a "post-date" questionnaire so that Dai, Dong, and Jai could assess their affective and motivational evaluations of their dating partner and the conversations they had with her. In order to determine how much the participants liked their partner, they were asked to rate on a scale of one to seven how positively or negatively they felt about their speed dating partner (1 = very negative, 7 = very positive) and how much they enjoyed the speed dating experience as a whole (1 = not at all, 7 = very much).

In order to determine how much participants desired their partner, they were first asked whether they wanted to talk to their partner again (yes or no). If they answered yes, they were subsequently asked to rate how strongly they desired to speak to their partner again (1 = very weakly, 7 = very strongly). If a participant answered "no" to the first question, his answer to the second question was automatically rated at "0."

Next, participants were asked how motivated they would feel to make a good impression on their dating partner, if they were given a chance to talk to her again (1 = not at all motivated, 7 = highly motivated). Finally, participants were asked to rate their impression of their speed dating partner (1 = extremely unfavorable, 7 = extremely favorable) and to assess how well they thought they would get along with this partner if they were to go on another date (1 = not at all, 7 = extremely well). Finally, participants were asked about how they perceived the warmth of the confederate.

As in the first study, participants in the easy-to-get condition found the player far more likeable than those in the hard-to-get condition. As in the first study, this was true regardless of whether the participant was in the commitment or no-commitment category.

When participants had no commitment towards their dating partner, they were more motivated to pursue a relationship with the partner who was employing the easy to get strategy; however, when the participants had establish some prior commitment to their dating partner, they were more inclined to pursue a relationship with the player who was employing the hard to get strategy.

Thus, the results of Dai, Dong, and Jai's second study were completely consistent with the results of their first study. In a real-world dating context, playing hard to get does hurt a player's likeability; however, given the existence of a prior psychological commitment, playing hard to get will make player seem more attractive to a potential romantic partner.

As long as the person you wish to attract is even a little bit mentally committed to you, playing hard to is, in fact, a highly effective dating strategy.

Using Reverse Psychology to Attract a New Romantic Partner

By this point you are thoroughly versed in what reverse psychology is and how it may be applied to the context of romantic attraction. You know that science has proven that you can use reverse psychology (by playing hard to get) in order to attract a member of the opposite sex.

Though you may have picked up some general ideas about how to effectively play hard to get by reading the previous sections, this chapter will walk you through everything you need to do in order to use reverse psychology to attract any romantic partner you desire!

Step 1: Establishing Commitment

Before you start playing hard to get, you need to make sure that your desired partner is psychologically committed to you.

This may sound daunting, but, as you may have gathered from Dai, Dong, and Jai's study, it doesn't actually take much to establish a basic level of psychological commitment. Let's assume you see an attractive guy or girl across the bar—someone you've never met before in your life. How do you get them to be psychologically committed to you?

Above all else, you want to be charming. Charm is something every single person is capable of using in order to get their foot in the door with the person you want to attract. There are some who confuse charm with manipulation, but manipulation is a form of exploitation that often involves lying and misdirection. Charm is something very different.

Being charming means making yourself look good by highlighting your strengths and using the tools of societal interaction to their maximum effectiveness. Charm simply makes you look good and attractive while you're in the process of building a genuine, healthy relationship. And don't worry—everyone can be charming! It just takes a little know how and a little practice.

<u>Assess the Situation</u>

Before you make your first move, you need to assess the situation so that you have some idea what you're dealing with. Do you already know someone the person you're interested in knows? Can you offer a good reason for introducing yourself? What signals is the other person's body language giving off?

You need to be able to answer all of these (and similar) questions beforehand in order to make the best first impression possible. Charm is all about coming in at the right angle at the right speed, and these factors differ with every new person in every new situation.

First, you need to figure out who your desired partner is. If you don't know, try to find out. Ask around, scope out some information from a mutual friend—you can even try to stalk his or her Facebook if you have to. Whenever possible, you want to learn his or her name in advance so that you can more easily remember it once you've been formally introduced. People love it when you remember their name.

The more information you can find out in advance, the better. Try to find out what they do for a living or some of the things they're interested in so that you can have some good questions to ask them once you do begin speaking with them. Obviously, you may not be able to do this if the person you wish to attract is a stranger at a bar, but whenever possible, try to casually gather as much intel as you can.

Next, you need to scan his or her body language. Nothing is less attractive than interrupting someone or bugging them when they just want to left alone. It's not hard to tell when someone isn't interested in talking to you. If someone is engaged in a conversation with other people, it's also probably a bad time to insert yourself into the fray.

One trick is to look at a person's feet as you approach in order to tell what type of conversation they're having. If only their torsos turn towards you, they're in the middle of an important conversation and you shouldn't interrupt them. If they turn both their feet and their torsos towards you, it's more likely that you're welcome to jump in.

You should never approach anyone who is talking or texting on her phone, wearing headphones, or generally looks unhappy, as you probably won't make a very good impression.

Make an Impression
Once you've analyzed the situation, you can begin to actually try to get the attention of the person you've been assessing. There are a number of subtle steps you can take in order to get them to notice you. One of the easiest and least risky signals

you can give is the eyebrow flash. This is a non-sexual advance that works equally well to attract the attention of both sexes.

You can also give them a brief glance—about four seconds will do. After the four second glance, look away, and then look back once again. Four seconds may seem like an unnervingly long time to stare at someone you've never even talked to before, but glancing at someone for anything less than four seconds risks seemingly like a casual look rather than a meaningful glance.

You should also smile a little. Most people believe that the smile is the most attractive thing about a potential partner, as a smile transforms the rest of your features and makes you seem like a happy person who is fun to be around. Since you'll be playing hard to get later, you may want to avoid being too smiley, but throwing a few smiles at your desired partner in order to get their attention certainly won't hurt you at this stage.

If your desired partner seems to be noticing your glances and smiles, you can then begin to (subtly!) mirror his or her body language. It's true what they say about imitation being the highest form of flattery, and when you imitate your desired partner's body language, you're already beginning to imply that the two of you share some kind of a connection.

Make sure you position your body so that you're mirroring the stance of the person you're interested in, but don't copy his or her every move—you don't want to appear weird or unnerving!

If things are still going well, now's the time to strike up a conversation. Though you don't want to say anything too trite or too forward, you should worry more about looking and sounding confident as you say it. Studies have shown that in a first impression, people tend to remember you based 70 percent upon how you appeared, 20 percent upon how you sounded, and only 10 percent upon what you said. You should, therefore, always pay close attention to your body language and your demeanor.

You'll want to have a reason you can offer as for why you're introducing yourself to them. This isn't a difficult thing to do; however, it's of paramount important, as it will imbue your interaction with a sense of purpose. Don't forget—you'll be playing hard to get with them soon, so you don't want to let on immediately that you're approaching them because you think they're attractive.

Try something more ambiguous—you could, for example, let them know that you find them interesting for one reason or another. If you're clear enough about your purpose, you'll also ensure that you'll have something to talk about and prevent any awkward, impression-ruining silences. Once you have your reason in mind, you should approach the person you're interested in with a confident smile. Your smile will subconsciously show that person you're not a threat while simultaneously demonstrating that you're confident with your environment and current situation.

If you're not sure how to smile confidently, practice what's known as the "Duchenne Smile"—push your cheeks up and squint your eyes slightly (try saying the word "cheeks" or any word that ends in "uh" if you're still not sure how to do this).

Smile often, but not excessively. You want to make a good impression, but you still shouldn't come off as over-eager, as this could hamper your strategy later on.

The Art of Conversation

Once you've finally made your introduction, be sure to continue being extra polite and engaging. Ask a lot of questions too. Questions are not only the best way to get to know someone—they're also the most effective tool you have when it comes to being charming. People love to talk about themselves almost as much as they love to know that other people are interested in them.

Don't waste any time—immediately signal that you want to get to know the person you want to attract. The trick is simply to not let onto them that you want to get to know them in a romantic context.

The possible questions you can ask are almost infinite. Anything that isn't too personal will work perfectly. For example, you might ask a person at a bar what brings her there tonight or what he's drinking. From there, you could ask their opinion about the establishment or where they're from. Whatever your questions are, make sure they're broad and easy to answer. If you make the right approach, you'll have plenty of time to ask more probing questions later. For now, asking general questions will allow you to approach in a way that's both likeable and memorable.

One easy way to appear even more likeable is to show that you are very much focused on the person you're talking to by being attuned to his or her speech and body language. If you make it clear that you're tuned in to whomever you're talking to, you'll give that person the impression that you're an engaging, thoughtful conversational partner.

First of all, take careful note of her name and use it at least a few times in the course of conversation. In addition, keep offering subtle reminders that you're engaged in the conversation. Make sure that you're as concerned with listening as you are with talking. Another important thing to remember is to be relatively positive.

Again, you don't want to appear overly positive or cheerful as you'll soon be playing hard to get, but when you're trying to first engage your desired partner, you'll want to be conscious of your choice of language. By speaking somewhat positively, you will maintain an open, inviting posture, an attractive tone of voice, and an animated, also attractive facial expression—all traits that will immediately draw someone to you.

Once you've spoken a little with the person you want to attract, it's not a bad idea to introduce them to someone (a wingman works well here) as your new friend. There are a lot of benefits to this trick. First, it will force you to remember his name. Second, it makes it seem like you know a lot of people, which makes you look even better. Third, calling them your friend signifies that the two of you already have a connection, but your romantic attraction to them remains ambiguous—which is exactly what you need it to be. You will be able to use this ambiguity to your advantage later on.

This step doesn't have to be complicated—when your friend walks up to you, all you need to do is say something like "Hey, Jim, this is my new friend Chelsea. Have you guys met yet?" This is one of those cases where having a wingman will undeniably work in your favor. That way, once you'd introduced him to your new "friend," he can say nice things about you. Maybe he doesn't know as much about being charming as you now do, so his presence alone could make you look better. The less charming he seems, the more you'll stand out!

As you continue to chat with your new "friend," keep an eye out for any shared interests. There is always at least a little common ground shared between any two people, so you should do your best to find it. As you're looking, keep an ear out for "latch" words—words you hear them say that match with your own interests. These are the words you should use to build more conversation with the person you want to attract.

For example, if you're a music lover, you should listen for words like "music" and "band" and use them to segue into further stories or questions. Don't interrupt when you hear them say a latch word. Simply bank as many of these words as you can in your memory as you listen to your desired partner speak. That way, you'll have a mental list of all the things you can talk about with them later—you'll have no more need to worry about awkward silences!

Make Yourself Memorable

One of the best things you can do to leave a good impression on someone is to make them feel like you understand them. Everyone wants to be understood and be accepted, so you'll do well to show that you empathize with them and their experiences.

Finding commonalities—as you will at this point already have begun to do—is the key to developing a solid emotional connection. In order to seem empathetic, you first need to build a sense of familiarity. This doesn't mean you need to over-share any information—and you shouldn't, given your later strategy—or ask overly personal questions.

Nevertheless, you need to get to know the person you wish to attract on a level that's not strictly factual. In order to do this, you might try asking them how they feel about certain aspects of their interests or asking what their passion is in life (and why they're passionate about it, etc.). In order for this to be most effective, you want to come off as open yourself. Drop some of the facades you may put on with other people you talk to and show a hint of vulnerability and humility.

The trick is to seem relatively (again—not overly) agreeable, without obviously contradicting your own beliefs. You want to bring yourself to your desired partner's level, whatever that level may be.

Always remember to mind your manners. Unfortunately, this is so rare anymore that just acting polite throughout a conversation can put you at a huge advantage and make you that much more memorable. Prioritize their interests over yours, and whatever you do, don't just "cut to the chase."

Don't ever interrupt a person when they're speaking. Try to turn off that voice in your head that has you thinking about what you're going to say next. Just listen to them and—more importantly—them her. You shouldn't just be waiting for your turn to talk. Don't be afraid to answer whatever questions they ask you, but don't spend too much time talking about yourself.

Be polite and honest and never give away too much information about yourself. Once you've answered, ask them another question. Never be pushy—if you feel like your question may be too intense, follow it with something like "if you don't mind me asking" in order to make them feel more comfortable.

Try to refrain from too much flattery—remember, you don't want this person to know that you're attracted to them yet. Compliments like "you have a great" sense of humor, however, can work in your favor without giving too much away.

If your conversation has been going well, you may want to consider employing touch at this point. Touch is such an important part of human interaction and as such it can be a great tool for making a winning impression.

You may be intimidated by the idea of incorporating touch, but when done correctly, a nonsexual touch can influence a person's behavior, increase the chances that he or she will comply with you, and make the person doing the touching seem friendlier and more attractive. Touch offers a physical affirmation of acceptance—as long as you don't take it too far. Stick to safe zones such as the upper back and the outside of the arms.

Sealing the Deal

Since you know you want to see this person again in the future, you need to get their phone number. As the conversation winds down, let them know that you've enjoyed the conversation and would like to speak again sometime. Whatever you do, do *not* imply that you have anything romantic in mind here.

Keep things casual. You could propose doing something involving the mutual interests you've established, or, you could keep it classically vague and suggest that you might like to "hang out sometime." Then, simply ask for their phone number. Once they give it to you—and if you've made a good enough impression they will give it to you—smile and thank them. Let them know that you look forward to speaking with them again soon.

As soon as you've gotten their phone number, it's time to stop working on establishing their psychological commitment to your\ (at this point, this stage should be complete!) and start playing hard to get, so you want to keep thing general and ambiguous.

On this note, you don't want to give them your phone number unless they specifically ask for it. You want to remain in control of the situation as much as possible. Don't ever make yourself too available.

Finally, don't linger. You'll want to keep the conversation moving at a brisk (though comfortable) pace. Don't cut the conversation short if things are going well, but don't drag it out either. When the pace of the conversation begins to die down, that's your cue to bail.

As you depart, you need to make sure whoever you just met will remember you. No matter how charming you were and how good of an impression you made, it won't matter if they don't remember you, so you need to do or say something unique in order to make sure they remember you and how likable you were.

Of course, it's important to be pleasant and tell them how nice it was to meet them, but do something to set yourself apart from everyone else they've met. Making a joke about something you've just discussed is an excellent way to do this.

If you can't think of anything witty, just touch them on the shoulder and let them know how much you enjoyed speaking with them. As long as you're not too weird, anything even slightly different from the norm will leave her with a positive impression—which is exactly what you want.

Once you make someone realize that there is depth to your character, they will be left curious about you, and you will begin to occupy their thoughts.

Step 2: Playing Hard to Get

If you've taken the above steps, you've already planted the seeds of attraction. Your desired partner may not be ready to drop to their knees for you just yet, but by this point you can be sure that they're intrigued by you.

Once someone begins to think of you in a particular way, they're likely to keep thinking of you in that same way. Now, you simply have to prove your worth, and a crucial part of proving your worth involves demonstrating that you're not too easy to get.

The Waiting Game

After you've established a psychological commitment with the person you wish to attract, it's imperative that you wait several days before you make any further contact with them.

Deep down, most people yearn for affirmation. Once someone has received a little attention—without any clear affirmation or rejection—from you, they will begin to have an interest in receiving your affirmation. Remember the uncertainty principle: people are most attracted to those who are potentially uninterested in them.

When the person you wish to attract does not hear from you for a few days, they will begin wondering whether or not you like them enough to want to pursue any kind of a relationship with them.

Towards the end of this waiting period, their deep-seated insecurities will begin to surface, and they will begin to find themselves yearning for your affirmation. By simply reaching out to contact them, you will be providing them with the affirmation they have been subconsciously seeking. This will only serve to further their psychological commitment to you.

Avoiding the Friend Zone

When you do finally make contact, you want to continue keeping the nature of your interest ambiguous. Men and women both have come to be terrified of ending up in what is known as "the friend zone," a term used to describe a situation where one of two "friends" has an unrequited attraction to the other.

In recent years, much has been of getting stuck in the friend zone whence escape is neigh impossible, but the simple fact is that you can employ reverse psychology to avoid ever getting stuck in the friend zone in the first place.

In order to avoid being categorized as a friend, all you have to do is make them think you've classified *them* as a friend. You can do this as you first begin to get to know the person you're attracted to by telling them that you think they'll make a really great friend. In so doing, you will make them think that you are disqualifying yourself as a potential romantic partner and therefore are unobtainable to them—this will promote a reactance response and make them feel as though they simply have to have you as more than just a friend.

Attractive men and women both come to be pretty used to getting hit on, so when someone new hits on them, they tend to write it off. They certainly don't find being hit on novel or interesting. This has a lot to do with something called the scarcity principle—when something isn't readily available, it seems more valuable and desirable.

The converse of this is also true, so when potential suitors are available to someone in abundance, that person doesn't typically place a lot of value on one more person who's hitting on them.

Therefore, counterintuitive as it may be, you can do well by disqualifying yourself as a potential suitor by implying that you think of the person you (secretly) wish to attract as nothing more than a friend.

Since everyone else is attracted to them, you will also leave them wondering why you aren't attracted to them and they will see it as a challenge to make you find them attractive, which means that they will find themselves trying to attract *you*.

By making it seem as though you are not attracted to them, you will also set yourself apart from the masses who are attracted to them and in so doing you will make yourself seem like a person of high value—this is a trait that tends to be attractive in and of itself. Because you are unique in your (implied) lack of romantic attraction for them, you will seem like a catch.

By making yourself out to be uninterested in a romantic or sexual relationship with someone you're actually attracted to, you will not actually be hindering your chances of achieving a romantic or sexual relationship with them. If anything, you will actually be making it more likely that he or she will be attracted to you. Once you establish a rapport with them, you can slowly begin to subtly flirt with them every once in a while.

Sending Mixed Signals

At this point, it's important that you remember the latch words you mentally banked during your first conversation. Everyone loves knowing that someone is paying a great deal of attention to them, so now's a good time to begin finding personal ways to compliment them that have nothing to do with their appearance and everything to do with their interests.

After a little while you should begin showing that you're interested in them, but you should by no means at this point let them know that your interest is of a romantic nature. You could, for example, send her a text in which you casually mention that she was in your dream the other night; however, you need to limit the details and keep the story and conversation moving. They doesn't need to know that your dream was actually a fantasy.

All you need to do is let them know that they occasionally enters your thoughts when they're not around. Once you do this, you can guarantee that they'll be thinking about you too. Remember, once people find themselves thinking about someone frequently enough, they naturally begin to find themselves attracted to the person who's been occupying so many of their thoughts.

The trick at this point is to send some signs of attraction, but not enough to demonstrate clear attraction. Mixed signals are key. You want to keep them guessing without raising any red flags that you're just another one of their many suitors. In conversation, maintain that you're their friend, but don't let your "friendship" stop you from flirting and teasing them. If you can do this, they will continue to see you as a person of high value and they will be all the more determined to attract you.

Maintaining Uncertainty

Remember, in order to attract someone to you, you need to make sure that they're constantly thinking about you without them knowing that you're constantly thinking about them too. The best way to do this is to make them think that you are potentially uninterested in them as a potential romantic partner.

Concealing your genuine desires is, ironically, a strategy which has been proven to have vastly better results than revealing those desires outright. In order to do this, you need to be in control of the situation. Any time the person you're interested in makes an advance, handle it ambiguously.

In fact, whenever they ask you a question, you should be as vague as possible without seeming outright sketchy. Remember, a little mystery is intriguing and intriguing is attractive. You want to keep the person you're interested in asking questions so that they actively desire to find out more about you.

The trick here is to be elusive without seeming shady—answer their questions, but give no more information than you have to. Leaving out details—especially details having to do with how you feel about the person you're talking to—will make you seem mysterious, which is a critical part of effectively playing hard to get.

If you don't give away every detail, they'll find themselves all the more compelled to get to know you better. If they ask how your weekend was, for example, all you need to say is that you hung out with some friends and had fun. Don't give them the full rundown. You want to leave them wondering who your friends were and what you guys did for fun. By doing this you'll secure yourself an even larger place in their mind.

Make Yourself Scarce

Once you've finally initiated contact, the person you're trying to attract will obviously have your phone number, which means that they will be able to call and text you. Don't make yourself too available.

Don't doge their calls, but don't jump to answer every time the phone rings either. If you're particularly committed to playing hard to get, you can try texting them immediately after she calls you. In your text, simply ask them what's up. That way, she'll be left wondering what (or who) you're spending your time on and why it's more important to you than picking up her calls. The idea that something is keeping you from them will only make them want you more.

If they text you, don't reply immediately. You may have been sitting there waiting for their text, but they certainly don't need to know that. Remember, desperation and being too "easy to get" is not remotely attractive to anyone who's the least bit committed to you, so make it seem like you're preoccupied with other things and can't answer right away.

There's no need to make them wait for an excessive period of time—this is rude and can make it obvious that you're trying to play hard to get. Instead, simply make them sweat it out for approximately 30 minutes before sending your reply. By that point, they're sure to be wondering what you're doing and why you're not answering—and, perhaps subconsciously, they'll find you that much more intriguing than they would if they knew every detail.

If they invite you to do something, you should carefully maintain this air of ambiguity without declining outright as a cold or blunt rejection could risk smoldering any spark you've managed to strike.

Instead, when they ask you to hang out on Friday night, tell them you have to do something for work and you're not sure your boss will let you out of it. They'll spend all week wondering whether or not she'll see you on Friday—and when Friday rolls around and you finally text them to let her know that your boss did, in fact, let you out of your obligation, they'll be elated to see you. They will actually cherish your time together more because it wasn't guaranteed to them.

<u>Make Them Chase You</u>
When you finally do see the person you wish to attract, you need to keep giving them reasons to chase you. At this point, they should be showing some signs of attraction to you. Your job is to play these up without betraying your own attraction to them.

A good way of doing this is asking them to qualify themselves to you. When done correctly, this will make it seem as though they're in a competition and you're the prize. Once it's quite obvious that the person is considering you as a potential romantic partner, you should begin ask questions such as "What makes you more interesting than the other people I've dated?" or

"What are three things you think I should like about you—excluding looks?"

If you keep your tone light enough and ask these kinds of questions in a joking, slightly flirty, almost sarcastic way, there's no way anyone will be able to resist being drawn in to the conversation. At this point, not only will you know that you're on their mind as a potential romantic partner, you'll also know that they feel that they have to earn their way into a relationship with you. Because you're making their goal of relationship formation moderately difficult, they'll be all the more motivated to "win" your attraction.

The so-called "three day rule" (waiting three days before contacting someone after hanging out) is coming to be dated and if you employ it, it may make it obvious that you're trying to play hard to get. Still, you shouldn't make yourself immediately and constantly available. This means that you occasionally need to say "no" when your desired partner asks you out—especially if you two have already spent some time that week.

Do not by any means make it look as if you are explicitly rejecting them—you simply want to make it look as though you have other plans as a reminder to the person you're interested in that they are not the center of your universe.

On a subconscious level, this may make them wish that they were the center of your universe. If nothing else, making them wait a little while before you see each other again will enhance their anticipation of seeing you and make them want to see you even more than they otherwise may have. You will ensure that you are on their mind, which is exactly where you want to be.

After a few weeks of playing hard to get, you can finally ask them out on a casual date. If you've successfully followed the steps outlined so far in this chapter, there's no way they'll turn you down. In fact, by this point you may not have to be the one to ask them on a date—you may simply be able to "yield" to their advances!

<u>Take Things Slow</u>

Even though you will have secured a date with the person you wish to attract, it's important that you continue to play a little hard to get. As far as the date itself goes, this is one situation where you absolutely do not want to hook up on the first date. Instead, you want to leave the person you wish to attract wanting more. Instead of going all the way right away, tease them a little bit. Slow your pace and draw things out—this is sure to drive them crazy and make them want you to give them what you've been holding back.

Even after you have had some kind of physical contact, don't immediately let them know how attractive you find them or how much you like them. Again—remember the uncertainty principle. People are more attracted to someone when they don't know how attractive that person finds them. Withholding some physical contact will continue to make your level of attraction unclear.

Once you've been on an official date, one final way to increase their attraction to you is to occasionally engage in some (harmless) flirting with others. This takes some nuance—you don't want to take it too far and actually hook up with someone else.

All you need to do is be a little flirty with other people when you're out in public with the person you wish to attract. Laugh at someone else's jokes or touch them gently on the arm when they're talking. Your potential romantic partner definitely take notice and it's likely that at this point that they'll be more than a little jealous. The more the person you want to attract feels they have to fight for your attention, the more they will value it when you do finally devote it to them.

If a relationship is in fact your goal, all you have to do now is slowly allow them to talk you into monogamy. That's the beauty of attracting someone using reverse psychology—after you take a few initial steps, you'll have them trying to attract *you*!

One Night Stands

Maybe you don't want a relationship with the person you wish to attract. If you just want to get them home for a night, that's fine—reverse psychology will work in that situation too!

If you're a woman, you can do this with relative ease. You should be able to follow the steps outlined above in order to establish a psychological commitment with the man you wish to attract. Then, start flirting with him—just a little bit. Don't make your interest too obvious. When he begins to flirt back, make it appear as if you are uninterested. Spurn any initial advances. Men love the idea of a chase—he'll be begging you back to his place in no time. All you'll have to do is eventually "concede."

For men, this process is a bit more involved. Women tend to be have more options for potential romantic partners and they also tend to be more selective in their choice of partner. You can use reverse psychology in order to get her to choose you for the night, but you'll have to employ a bit of nuance.

In order to do this, you can take advantage of the societal stigma known as "slut-shaming." Men are generally able to have sex with whomever they want without having to fear any kind of repercussion from society at large. In fact, they may actually enhance their social worth by participating in such behavior. Women who freely have sex with whomever they desire, however, quickly earn the label "slut" or "whore." These women are then scorned by society because they are "easy"—they'll sleep with anyone.

Obviously, men tend to see no harm in this situation. In fact, many see themselves as benefitting from it, as when they choose a woman to marry, they'll know that she will have likely had no more than a few sexual partners. Women, however, tend to dislike this stigma. It's discriminatory against them, and many find themselves sexually frustrated. Fear of the way in which they will be perceived by society often prevents a woman from having sex with a man "too soon," even if they find the man quite desirable.

Because women are afraid of being labeled as a slut, they have a tendency to put up barriers that some men find impossible to wear down. Most women find society's attitude towards their sexuality annoying; however, they typically believe that they have no choice but to deal with their frustration in silence, as society tends to be structured in such a way that it favors men. Their mentality provides you with the perfect opportunity to employ reverse psychology on them.

Most men simply ignore the way societal bias prohibits a woman's sexual freedom; however, it is advantageous for you to come right out and acknowledge the fact that men have it better than women when it comes to being able to sleep with whomever they want. Next, you should state that you dislike this status quo because you feel that it is discriminatory towards women.

Finally, ask the woman her opinion on the matter—does she feel that she faces discrimination for her sexuality? In the first step, you are essentially priming the woman you desire by conveying to her that you are honest and confident—it's unlikely that any man will have said this to her before.

By explicitly taking her side (and the side of the discriminated party generally) in the second step, you will naturally endear yourself to her. In the third step, you put her a position where it's hard to disagree with you—after all, she more than likely will by this point already find you honest, confident, and decent.

Once she agrees with you, she will naturally begin to start thinking about having sex with you, even if she hadn't even considered the possibility before. Society has impressed upon her that sleeping with a man before taking the time to carefully consider him as a partner makes her a slut; however, you have reverse this principal in her mind.

After speaking with you, she will inevitably feel that she is backing up a discriminatory position against herself by not being willing to sleep with any man she likes. It will occur to her that sleeping with you is a good way to rebel against the societal discrimination she has experienced.

Basically, you're making it known to her that it's societally "forbidden" for her to have sex with you, and in so doing, you will activate within her a feeling of reactance. Not only will she suddenly find herself wanting to have sex with you, she'll believe that having sex with you is the perfect way to rebel against the society by which her options were limited.

Using Reverse Psychology to Re-Attract Your Ex

It may not be something you want to think about while you're dreaming of attracting a great new partner, but what happens if the two of you should someday break up? Can you use reverse psychology to attract them back to you in much the same way that you used reverse psychology to win them over initially? Absolutely!

On the most basic level, you simply need to understand what your ex expects you to do after the breakup. Whatever this is, you should then do the opposite. Eventually, your ex will realize that they have made a mistake by letting you go. Reverse psychology, as you probably will have gleaned by this point, works best on those who are in a highly emotional, likely anti-confirmative state, so after a breakup, your ex will almost definitely qualify.

So what, exactly does your ex expect you to do after a breakup? This will of course vary from situation to situation, but some expectations are rather general. First of all, they'll likely expect you to be in a highly emotional state too, especially since you're the one who was just broken up with. It may be hard, but don't make a scene. Do not cry, scream, or anything of the sort. From the moment the breakup happens, you need to appear calm, composed, and mature. Do not let on that the breakup has affect you, no matter how heartbroken you feel.

Your ex will probably expect you to call them numerous times within the first few days of your breakup, begging them to take you back. This, unfortunately, is somewhat natural to do after you've just been dumped. But you want to use reverse psychology—you want to defy their expectations.

This means you do not contact them. At all. No calls, no texts, no emails, and whatever you do, do not try to see them in person. If they try to get in touch with you during these first few days, do not respond. Remember, for those who have even the slightest commitment to you, being easy to get is not at all attractive.

It may take a few days for the weight of your silence to really impact your ex, but once it does, their head will be reeling. After all, they expected to have gotten at least a dozen calls from you by now, so what happened?

Internally, they'll begin to experience some doubt. Maybe they didn't know you as well as they thought they did. Maybe you really weren't that into them to begin with. Maybe you're even happy to now be broken up. Cue a reactance response.

Your ex will find that they are thinking of you more and more. Even though your ex broke up with you, they'll begin to feel as though they couldn't have you even if they wanted to. You will have once again become a scarce—and therefore valuable—commodity in their eyes, just as you appeared to be when you first tried to attract them.

Given that they have been subtly reminded of just how valuable you are, they will inevitably begin to feel as though they have made a mistake in ending your relationship. The longer your ex goes without hearing from you, the more frequently they will experience these thoughts about what they might be missing out by having dumped you.

Before too long, they'll reach out to you to see if you're really as uninterested in them as you seem. Maintain that you're content with the breakup and doing just fine. This will prompt them to spend more and more time wondering if they made a mistake by letting you go—and as you know well, people correlate frequent thoughts about a person with being attracted to that person.

Before long, they'll be asking you to take them back. All you'll have to do is concede.

A Final Word

This book has attempted to cover a significant amount of ground. Now that you've completed it, you should know how reverse psychology works, how it applies to the context of attraction, and how you can effectively use it to win the attraction of a member of the opposite sex.

After reading this book, you should absolutely feel ready to go out and attract a member of the opposite partner by playing hard to get. You will also, however, likely have an increased appreciation for the intricate and complex nature of human psychology.

Everyone is different and, as such, everyone's minds work slightly differently. You should not expect reverse psychology to work in absolutely every scenario.

You may be confident, however, that if you follow the guidelines given to you in this book, using reverse psychology to attract a member of the opposite sex will work for you in the majority of scenarios.

Printed in Great Britain
by Amazon